JUDY MASTRANGELO

INSPIRATIONAL VISIONS

ORACLE CARDS

REDFeather
MIND | BODY | SPIRIT

4880 Lower Valley Road, Atglen, PA 19310

Copyright © 2020 by Judy Mastrangelo

Library of Congress Control Number: 2020930550

All rights reserved. No part of this work may be reproduced or used in any form or by any means—graphic, electronic, or mechanical, including photocopying or information storage and retrieval systems—without written permission from the publisher.

The scanning, uploading, and distribution of this book or any part thereof via the Internet or any other means without the permission of the publisher is illegal and punishable by law. Please purchase only authorized editions and do not participate in or encourage the electronic piracy of copyrighted materials.

"Red Feather Mind Body Spirit" logo is a trademark of Schiffer Publishing, Ltd.
"Red Feather Mind Body Spirit Feather" logo is a registered trademark of Schiffer Publishing, Ltd.

Designed by Brenda McCallum

Type set in Romance Fatal/Minion
ISBN: 978-0-7643-6000-8
Printed in China

Published by Red Feather Mind, Body, Spirit
An imprint of Schiffer Publishing, Ltd.
4880 Lower Valley Road
Atglen, PA 19310
Phone: (610) 593-1777; Fax: (610) 593-2002
E-mail: Info@schifferbooks.com
Web: www.redfeathermbs.com

For our complete selection of fine books on this and related subjects, please visit our website at www.schifferbooks.com. You may also write for a free catalog.

Schiffer Publishing's titles are available at special discounts for bulk purchases for sales promotions or premiums. Special editions, including personalized covers, corporate imprints, and excerpts, can be created in large quantities for special needs. For more information, contact the publisher.

Author Note; I would like to thank my editor, Dinah Rosberry, for all of her wonderful advice, help, and encouragement in the creation of this oracle deck. And many thanks also to Brenda McCallum for doing such a beautiful job in designing it.

To my dear and talented husband, Michael,
for all of his love and encouragement.

CONTENTS

Introduction	6
Using the Cards	8
Mind Painting	10
The Secret Sanctuary	12
The Method	12
Oracle Cards	19

1 Alice and the White Rabbit	20	7 Dogwood Fairy	32
2 Ariel	22	8 Elf Scribe	34
3 Bunny Gardener	24	9 Eternal Spirit	36
4 Celestial Cherub	26	10 Excalibur	38
5 Create Your Fantasy	28	11 Fairy Honeymoon	40
6 Dance to the Music	30	12 Fairy Swan Ride	42
		13 Fairy-Tale Folk	44

#	Title	Page
14	Fire Dragon	46
15	Flower Goddess	48
16	Flower Spirit	50
17	Garden of Unicorns	52
18	Gingerbread Witch	54
19	Guardian Spirit	56
20	Hansel & Gretel Lost in the Woods	58
21	Jack and the Giant	60
22	Journey of Fantasy	62
23	Knight and the Dragon	64
24	Land of Pegasus	66
25	Listen to the Spirits	68
26	Little Blossom Fairies	70
27	Lonely Dragon	72
28	Mad Hatter's Tea Party	74
29	Magical Lands	76
30	Merlin and Young Arthur	78
31	Moon Fairy Goddess	80
32	Morning Glory Fairy	82
33	Mounting Pegasus	84
34	Oberon and Titania	86
35	Pan and Unicorn	88
36	Paradise of Children	90
37	Peaceful Garden	92
38	Penguin Riding By	94
39	Puck's Magic Flower of Sleep	96
40	Share Some Joy	98
41	Sleeping Beauty	100
42	Teddy Bear Picnic	102
43	The Lovers	104
44	The Magic Flute	106
45	The Road to Oz	108
46	Touch of Angels	110
47	Tulip Fairy	112
48	Welcome to Make-Believe	114
49	Where Candy Trees Grow	116
50	Wizard of the Galaxy	118

INTRODUCTION

Imagination is the stuff that Dreams are made of. It has been the inspiration of poets, painters, composers, and great thinkers alike throughout the ages. Humankind the world over has ascended to great heights by developing their personal and individual means of expressing heartfelt feelings. This card deck is intended to help enhance the skill of imagination. By doing so, you can attempt to develop to your highest potential, using your own wonderful talents to the utmost.

Being able to express your deepest feelings can bring you great happiness. Life of course brings us all many ups and downs.

But we can use these experiences, both good and bad, to come to an understanding of ourselves. Through developing your imagination, you can "Paint a Mind Picture" of what you would like your ideal self to be. This will be the ultimate that you will strive for. We can all imagine ourselves to be Gods and Goddesses, Elves and Fairies, Wizards, and Nature Spirits.

This inspirational card deck can help encourage you to realize the person that you would like to become. Here you may discover abilities that you didn't even know you had. You will be encouraged to develop skills, such as through art, that will take your life to new heights and help you solve everyday problems. Sometimes these problems may seem insurmountable. But they needn't be.

Deep within your Soul lie many fantastic dreams and aspirations. Art forms, such as literature, painting, music, dance, etc. abound with the fantastic in the world of wizards, dragons, fairies, and magic. These beings symbolize our hopes and emotions. By using this deck, you can develop your own intuitive abilities to fulfillment and overcome the fear of trying new things. Everyone is born with individual and unique talents. Unfortunately many of us don't take the time to develop them. Well, now is your chance to do so!

Using the Cards

First close your eyes, and come to grips with how you feel at the moment. Do you need help with a very dire problem that needs immediate attention? Or would you like some inspiration to get you out of the doldrums of everyday life? Think of what answers you would like, and ask them to the ether.

Then meditate to find your own special way to use these cards. Let your own innate intuition be your guide. Try choosing what appears very special to you at the moment. You may find that it will be the very thing to uplift and inspire you at that specific moment.

This process you choose may change each time you use these cards, or you might find one individual way that always suits you best.

SOME SUGGESTIONS

Look deep inside your Soul to find your way.
Relax and feel your body attune with the world and all of nature.
Feel yourself letting go of pent-up tensions.
Touch your fingertips on both hands lightly together.
Concentrate on them, breathing deeply.
They may become sensitive and warm.

You may be self-directed to shuffle the cards, fan them out, or even just spread them all over the table. Be inspired. Relax your body as you pass your hands gently over the cards, feeling their vibrations. Your intuitive mind may direct you to select one or two cards. These will be your selection to guide you for inspiration and Enlightenment in this session.

Each card has its own special encouraging message under its title. For further information about each card, refer to the card section of this book. The descriptions found there will give you insight and suggestions about personal development. This is the knowledge that your inner self and your spirit guides have chosen to uplift you at this time.

You will become your own personal clairvoyant reader, since you know yourself the best. Your spirit guides are within you and around you, helping you always. They want the best for you. You just have to get used to contacting them. The greatness that is you will never be abandoned. It will just get better and better. Do not be afraid. Enjoy the excitement of it all!

Mind Painting

I feel that art is one of the highest expressions of humankind. Sometimes people think of the word "artist" as referring to mainly the "art of painting." But actually it refers to all of the "fine arts" of literature: painting, music, dance, drama, etc. There is also the "art of living." I've developed my method of "Mind Painting" in which I first see a "vision" of what I want to paint in my "mind's eye." Then I develop the vision into a painting, which I enjoy sharing with others. This method can also be used for any of the fine arts I've mentioned.

Many artists in the past have developed wonderful procedures along these same lines also. This method enhances one's ability to conceive of an initial vision of a work of art. It is very exciting and uplifting to visualize something out of one's imagination, and great painters, authors, music composers, dance choreographers, and dramatists of the past and present have used similar methods. It can be termed "inspiration."

Besides creating a "work of fine art," you can also "paint a picture" of your ideal self as you would *want* to be. This self-portrait could be of a "new you" that you can strive for. It can be yourself in the future, where you have become healthier by living an improved lifestyle. You could be developed creatively and intellectually, but still strive to better yourself along certain other lines that you admire in others. Sometimes you might think to yourself: "It's a shame I've never studied this or that. I always wanted to but never had the time." Well, you can strive to become whatever you aspire to be in the new Mind Painting of yourself that you create. Make your self-portrait as attractive as possible, showing and doing all the wonderful things that you've always wanted to do! You can paint yourself traveling to other countries, enjoying yourself with friends and family, walking out in nature, being with animals, and in short, doing and achieving all the things you've always wanted to do but never had the time or inclination to do. You might not even have had the courage to try to do them, because you felt you didn't have enough talent. I'm not saying that everyone can do everything. I myself love to dance, but I don't have the ability to become a professional dancer. But that never stands in my way when I want to dance, since I enjoy it very much. I've found my own little niche being a painter and author—which I love to do.

Everyone has talents they were born with. They can develop these wonderful gifts that make them unique to the best of their abilities. As I mentioned, besides the fine arts of literature, there is also the art of living. And if you don't have the desire to be an author, painter, composer, dancer, actor, etc., you might want to develop other arts, which are wonderful in themselves, such as the fine art of creating a garden, cooking, sewing, woodworking, healing arts, teaching, and many more. To be able to do something you love in the best possible way is truly a form of art.

The Secret Sanctuary

Now, when you have decided what kind of art you truly love and would like to create with a Mind Painting, let's decide where you would like to do it. That's really a very important decision.

You might want to make your own "secret sanctuary" where you can go to create when you find some time to yourself to meditate in your own little world. It could be a special room in your home where you can be alone and spend peaceful quiet time. You can enjoy decorating it with things that are beautiful and inspiring to you. A special corner of a garden or park that is comfortable and where you love to be is also an option. It can be mostly anywhere, even in a crowded place. Inspirational, original ideas can pop into your head at any time or place. You can daydream anywhere, including on a subway, car, or plane. (You just have to make sure you are doing it when you don't have to concentrate on other important things, such as driving a car, or crossing a street! But of course that goes without saying. It's always good to be a dreamer, but at the right time and place, so as not to endanger yourself or others.)

The Method

I've developed this method in order to enhance my ability to conceive of, and create, a painting. And you can use it too. It is a way to originate ideas and images for your artwork. The term "Mind Painting" can be applied to any kind of creative thinking.

It doesn't have to be a painting. You can use the same techniques I use for a painting, in order to do whatever is in your heart.

I first visualize an image and develop it in my mind over a period of time. I don't sketch it down with drawings. It's all in my head. I can see it with my eyes open or closed—in a daydream or at night before sleeping.

I usually practice this when I have some time to myself where I can relax and dream about my ideas. This could be during the daylight hours or at night before going to sleep. Closing your eyes is often helpful. Sometimes meditating on something, such as a flower, clouds, or water, is a good way to bring forth your imaginative "visions" from the beautiful treasures you store in your unconscious mind. This is similar to the method of "scrying," such as looking into a "crystal ball" to "see" what will appear. Then, when you start visualizing these amazing images, try to practice holding them as a "master image" in your mind. This image can serve as an inspiration for a new painting. Sometimes I write down the description of my Mind Painting, if I'm not able to remember it in its entirety.

Initially, an idea will come to me about something that I would like to create. It might be inspired by a beautiful flower, a sunset, or the amazing work of a great master artist. Then I relax and daydream in order to see images in my mind that I feel would best express my initial idea. It's similar to watching a wonderful movie when these imaginative pictures appear.

I was first aware of my inclinations to see imaginative visions when I was young. The trick was to be able to control the parade of these images and mold them the way I wanted. I had to focus my mind on the overall main image I was trying to develop—the image I wanted to use for a painting. At first these "Mind Pictures" were very fleeting and a bit chaotic. The images seemed to dance around in my mind. Sometimes they first appeared as abstract forms, which then magically transformed into amazing pictures. It's similar to your state of mind when you start to fall asleep, and dreams begin to appear. It's a type of "stream of consciousness" where your mind tries to depict the many thoughts flowing around inside your head. It can put you in a dreamlike trance state, and some might even term it channeling from the "beyond." I like to think of it as contacting my wonderful imagination, dreams, and ideas within me. In my case, they usually start off as fantastic images, which can coalesce into a wonderful vision for a painting, or series of paintings, which could also develop into an illustrated book idea.

Often, the use of stimuli, such as music that you love, will be a wonderful inspiration for creativity. Just close your eyes and listen to it as it creates amazing art forms in your mind. As I mentioned, I enjoy the art of dance very much and have done quite a bit of choreography. I've developed my Mind Painting abilities to the point where I can hear a piece of music and see an entire ballet being danced from start to finish, complete with wonderful dancers in brilliant costumes and fantastic scenery. What fun that is!

Sometimes I will gaze at beautiful paintings that I love, then close my eyes. I will see that painting evolve into many forms, as I sit back and enjoy the show. Great paintings are often very inspiring to me in my Mind Painting. I think all artists are influenced by their favorite great art that has come before them. They then evolve it further in their own personal way, adding their own heartfelt touches. I collect art books, calendars, prints, and greeting cards of my favorite artists. I put their art on my walls and carry small postcards and prints of their work with me so I can glance at them in my free time when I'm away from home. I steep myself with their brilliance, and they inspire me all the time. I am always learning from my artist friends of the past. If I'm stuck with a painting problem, I just go to them for advice. My questions are often answered by looking at their wonderful work. All of these things influence my Mind Paintings. And this can apply to any art form that you would like to develop as your own.

I might also think about a fairy tale or myth and yearn to illustrate it. I love the Renaissance era, mythical creatures, castles, etc. The art of film is another wonderful stimulus to imagination. I love fantasy movies, and seeing films such as *The Wizard of Oz*, *The Lord of the Rings*, *The Hobbit*, Harry Potter films, and the classic Disney animations are extremely inspiring. I envision them in my mind after I see them, and they live inside my heart to always inspire me to create my own artistic works.

I enjoy creating fantasy clothes for my figures in my paintings. "But how do I get ideas to design these clothes?" you might ask. Well, I collect interesting things, such as pieces of fabric, feathers, shells, etc., and I place them around my art studio. By using my imagination, I find the perfect things I need. I just see a Mind Painting in my mind and make fantastic creations out of the interesting little things I've collected.

Sometimes, rather than using a real outfit, I'll paint a figure in a costume made out of flowers, leaves, or other nature objects. I find that these lovely things are perfect clothes for elves and fairies, and flower petals flow just like beautiful fabric. I might use acorn tops for elfin caps and cups, and sit the Wee Folk on mushrooms. Interesting rocks can be used to resemble mountains. If I need a body of water, I can use a mirror to show reflections, or a shallow pan of water. All this may end up looking like a miniature train layout. When I paint a fantasy piece that I saw in a vision in my imagination, I'll then use my collection as a still life to draw from. I can create something amazing out of the very ordinary since I've developed my ability to dream.

When you develop your abilities to "dream" about little everyday things, they will stimulate ideas for you. I often see things in nature that inspire me for my artwork. Sometimes an idea just pops into my head as I go through my daily life. I might come across a wizened old tree that resembles a "creature" that I could use in my art. I could even get an idea for a fantastic landscape just by looking at clouds or at something as ordinary as bedsheets and blankets on a bed!

As I mentioned, the inspiration of Mind Painting in your imagination can light up like a lightbulb anywhere that you are. For example, one summer evening, I was walking in a meadow by moonlight. It was a very lovely and magical place. Suddenly, an idea for a painting came to me. In that very meadow, I envisioned fairies dancing with little rabbits, surrounded by glowing lightning bugs and mushrooms. After that wonderful night of inspiration, I later completed my painting, which I titled *Moonlit Dance*. I had seen it previously as a Mind Painting in my head, all completed, even before I sketched it on my canvas!

This technique can be developed to the point where an image will just pop into your head for a painting. It will show the completed painting, in color, down to the last detail. And this complete image is something you should try to keep with you as a model to strive to create, through all the stages of development.

I know of two famous artists who had interesting methods of capturing a vision to paint: Pablo Picasso was known to paint in a trancelike state. Salvador Dalí, the surrealist, would sit in a chair and hold a metal spoon with a metal pan under it next to his chair. When he would finally fall asleep, his hand would drop the spoon, and it would hit the pan with a loud clatter. That would wake him with a start, and he would be inspired to paint the dream images he was having before he awoke.

You too can develop your own process of inspiration for your art with your own version of Mind Painting.

Alice and the White Rabbit

Follow adventure down the rabbit hole.

Throw caution to the winds, and let your hair down. Join the Excitement of a new adventure.

Don't be afraid to try something new and thrilling. Keep your eyes open and protect yourself from mishaps, but enjoy every minute of the fun!

Ariel

Spirit Beings are everywhere.

Ethereal creatures are the soul of nature and are all around us. They live in trees, flowers, water, and air. Become close to nature to experience its great qualities, and be amazed at their beauty. You will never be alone if you contact these delicate beings. Be sensitive and kind to them, and they will return the favor.

Great artists throughout the ages have been inspired to create when contacting them. You can be also. If you open up your heart, you will see and hear them, just as William Shakespeare did in his depiction of Ariel:

> Where the bee sucks, there suck I:
> In a cowslip's bell I lie;
> Merrily, merrily shall I live now,
> Under the blossom that hangs on the bough.

Bunny Gardener

Home is where your spirit dwells.

Make your home a Sacred Sanctuary where you feel comfortable to relax and hang your hat. It should reflect your own personal tastes in every way. Create a beautiful environment where you can invite your friends in to visit for tea, and walk your garden paths.

Tending your beautiful flower beds is so healing, as you contact Mother Earth. And within your intimate cottage, make yourself a wonderful special room. You will be able to go there to do your exciting creative work, when inspiration beckons you.

Celestial Cherub

*Guardian Angels watch over us at night to make
sure our sleep is safe and sound.*

If you envision Angelic Beings in your mind, they will appear to you. They guard you always, giving you lovely inspirational dreams of fairy tales, and long-ago lands. Their lit candles are the sparkling stars you see in the sky at night.

These gentle Angels will give you hope through the darkness, no matter what your age. Believe in their goodness.

Create Your Fantasy

Feel the magic.

Imagine a world for yourself with everything you love, full of all your secret wishes. You can fill it with amazing creatures that don't even exist in our everyday life, such as unicorns, elves, and fairies. Wave a sparkling wand and make rainbows and castles appear in the sky. Talk to the animals. Become a royal prince or princess, or anyone else you want to be.

Paint a picture of your imaginary world in your mind, and on paper if you like. You can visit this beautiful kingdom whenever you like. It will uplift and inspire your life, and you can develop and expand it at anytime. Feel the magic of your new world.

Dance to the Music

Join in with the music and dances of nature.

Don't lose the ability to enjoy the beauty of music. Dance and sing to its melodies. It will give you great joy, and you will be uplifted.

Develop your imaginative powers with games such as these:

> Close your eyes, and feel your body becoming small
> and delicate as fluttering Butterflies, and Birds.
> Imagine yourself floating up higher and higher into the sky,
> as a lovely Fairy, flying in a Sunlit Day.
> Picture yourself sailing through the clouds, light as air.

Play your "game of imagining" often, and it will bring you great joy. Music has heavenly inspirational powers, so if you include moving and dancing to its lovely strains, it will enhance your beautiful experience of the art of living.

Dogwood Fairy

Take time to dream in the flowers.

You're feeling bogged down by the stress of our everyday modern lifestyle. So take a hint from the delicate sprightly fairies: Dream a while, taking in the beauty of life.

And don't forget to talk to the flowers. They love to listen.
Lady of the Dogwood Trees sits lightly on her floating blossoms, lost in sweet reverie. It is very soothing, relaxing, and rejuvenating to be like her.

Elf Scribe

The stories of the Wee Folk are delightful.

You also have many tales to tell. The art of writing is a wonderful mode of expressing your inner thoughts and aspirations. Dream on your feelings, to discover deep emotions. You may surprise yourself to discover the seeds of ideas that have slept inside your heart for years, waiting to grow and blossom out.

Transcribe your hidden secrets for posterity, and embark on a journey of self-discovery. Be an elf scribe:

> Write your tales throughout the night,
> beneath a glowing Bell Flower Light.

Eternal Spirit

Our souls live forever, so reach for the stars.

We all evolve from earthly roots, but we can soar on wings of butterflies to the heavens. We are a joyful combination of both earth and sky. Your inner being may strive for transcendental purity and visions, if you persevere in achieving your goals.

Never give up your "Mind Painting" of the ideal person you want to be. You will ascend if you believe in your great value.

Excalibur

Be strong and honest, and you will achieve your quest.

You too can be "king" or "queen" of the realm, if you stay resolute and follow your dream. Never swerve from your path to enlightenment.

King Arthur achieved greatness because he had the courage to pull the sword Excalibur from the stone. Then he dared to create a spiritual kingdom. And so can you. Believe in yourself, and others will also!

Fairy Honeymoon

Life can be eternal bliss when you love and are loved.

Every day can be a honeymoon, when you give love to your dear ones. To share your world with that special someone is one of the greatest gifts of joy you will ever receive. So open your heart to those you care about, and let them come inside your soul. This is a most priceless experience.

When elves and fairies marry,
They float on wings of love to live an eternal bliss,
In cloud castles, nestled amongst the moon and stars.

Fairy Swan Ride

Enjoy the company of others; it will fill your world with happiness.

Try new, fanciful things, and socialize with people you have fun being with. Even if you do this just once in a while, it's always a delight to be among good souls in an enchanting place. It gets the cobwebs out and brings sparkles into your life. Then write a poem or song to share with your friends, such as this one describing the joy you feel being with them:

> A graceful Swan Boat glides through quiet waters.
> Sing to me my little ones of lands where dreams are born.
> Sky dreams, cloud dreams, castles full of fairy tales, lands where elves dwell, and fairies dance till morn.

Fairy-Tale Folk

Remain friends with your childhood fantasies;
they will keep you young.

Express and share your heartfelt feelings and ideas by bringing fantasy creatures into being. Bring them to life by creating your own stories. Reach into your childhood memories and pull out your favorite storybook friends. What a joy that will be! They will appear to you, just as if you were watching a movie about them. You will see them talk and dance and fly—and everything else they like to do! Then you can paint a picture of them and write their stories down. They will be really real, once you bring them to life.

Civilizations throughout the world have always written their own fairy tales and myths. The creatures in these stories symbolize the deepest hopes and visions of humankind. Be creative!

Fire Dragon

Dragons live within our minds, and we must harness their fire.

Some days you may feel so angry about an event that you want to breath fire and brimstone and shout and cry, all at once! It's only human to be that way, because Life has many pitfalls. Venting your desperate emotions is healthy and important, but within boundaries, of course.

Begin by visualizing a "Mind Painting" of your angry fire dragon struggling to come out. Then do a real painting of your rage. Express yourself through dancing, piano playing, and singing. Pound some clay to create an expressive sculpture. When you're finished, take deep breaths, close your eyes, and softly relax. You will feel much better after expressing yourself. Try not to take out anger on yourself or others.

Flower Goddess

*Feel at one with nature,
and commune with all living beings.*

The world of flowers is such a magnificent one. Experience this fantastic land by immersing yourself in your garden. Become "the goddess of flowers," who communes with all her creatures, no matter how tiny. Befriend all the flittering butterflies, grass, and tiny insects, which will fill you with awe for the beauties of nature.

> Become the flower goddess,
> Who stands atop her boundless magic kingdom,
> In which an endless twilight river transports one to
> Worlds of inspiration, beyond imagination.

Flower Spirit

Lift your eyes up to the sun.

Rise from your silken-petaled bed of roses and greet the morning sun. Thank him for his life-giving gift of warmth and light to Earth.

Be grateful for all the wondrous things on Earth and beyond that humankind has the joy of experiencing. Celebrate life!

Garden of Unicorns

Hope lives in the darkness.

Never stop searching for a perfect world. It does exist somewhere, glowing brightly in the darkest corners of the universe. You just have to keep searching. Never give up hope of finding this beautiful garden oasis with its magic fountain of eternal life. Be like the ethereal unicorns who drink from it. This guiding light in moments of despair will uplift you.

Keep a "Mind Painting" of it deep within your heart, to bring you much happiness.

Gingerbread Witch

Don't be afraid of creatures from the dark side.

Throughout books and movies, we find characters who appear negative and evil. They are very familiar to you, represented by demons, dragons, and witches. As children, you might have feared them. When you grew older, you may have met people who seemed similar to these fantasy villains.

You must become strong and understand that these people are not to be feared. Have the strength to stand up to them and say to yourself: "I'm not afraid of you!" They then will seem less harmful and, on closer look, could even appear pathetic and even laughable. Always be brave and stand up for your rights. Do not be bullied. You are a wonderful and valuable person!

Guardian Spirit

Protector of your soul.

There is a celestial being who is always by your side to watch over you. You may not know they are there, but understand that they are faithful to you always.

Reach out to this higher power, who is your advocate in life. They lovingly bring you heavenly dreams of sublime worlds, to give you inspiration, hope, and happiness.

Hansel & Gretel Lost in the Woods

*Feeling lost can be frightening;
accept the help of a loved one to find your way home.*

When walking through the forest of life, as twilight colors deepen, you often become lost. Trees and roots can appear like evil menacing creatures, ready to pounce on you. Even though you scatter bread crumbs on the trail, you still might not be able to find the way home.

Reach out to take the hand of your dear brother or sister friend to help guide you through the forest maze, and back to warmth. Together you can help each other find your path again. You are not alone.

Jack and the Giant

Stand up tall and escape the giants.

Be brave and make a change in your life for the better. Escape the negatives that set up road blocks to your happiness and self-fulfillment. These obstacles make it very difficult to become your Ideal that you have "Mind Painted" and that you dream of becoming.

Picture yourself a hero who can overcome any adversity, so that you will be free to become the great person you are!

Journey of Fantasy

Use your imagination to create a world of delight.

Don't be shy. Enjoy the fun and fantasy of life. In literature, music, painting, and drama, there are many subjects that may seem unreal. That's the fun of it all! The topsy-turvy world that is sometimes portrayed in art could at first seem ludicrous. But on closer look, it might be quite thought provoking, and refreshingly captivating.

Try your hand at creating artwork, such as a story or painting, with subject matter that may seem ill matched. The result might surprise you and be very clever and entrancing. They say humor is the best medicine. Enjoy the world of creating!

Knight and the Dragon

Feel your power.

Stand up to battle the threatening dragons of life. These monstrous evil creatures come in many forms: wrongdoing, sickness, and untruths, to name a few. You are a superhero, so be not afraid to wear your shining armor to shield you from their ferocious blasts of fire.

If you have not been courageous in the past, now is the time to be the master of your fate. Exert an effort to become healthy in mind and body, so that you can defeat these monstrous and belligerent beasts. You will be glad to make a stand to right the wrongs and heal the world for yourself and others. You can do this through the strength of spirit and will. That is a true hero.

Land of Pegasus

Fantastic beasts do exist!

You are a poet, like those of long ago, who imagined amazing creatures, such as beautiful unicorns that could soar in the sky. They shared their songs of enchantment, which uplifted people beyond their everyday lives, to greater heights. And their songs also inspired others to create art themselves, expressing their dreams and personal feelings. It's such a fulfilling experience that you can develop in yourself!

Play this imagining game: Look outside into the sky, on a day with beautiful billowing clouds. Dream upon these lovely ever-changing puffs, and imagine what they become and look like to you. They may appear as castles, fantastic animals, or flying ships. Then close your eyes and see continuing sky visions, to see how they evolve. Be inspired to paint a picture in watercolors or words.

Listen to the Spirits

Be sensitive to the beings that surround you.

Your Guardian Spirits watch over you. They live both within your soul and all around you, often confiding secret knowledge of the spheres. Heed their gentle whispers, which might prove very helpful in solving your problems.

They also help fill your psyche with magnificent creative thoughts that will inspire you to greatness.

Little Blossom Fairies

Become friends with the fairies in your garden.

Surround yourself as much as possible with nature, for that is where the Little Folk live. Close your eyes to imagine finding them in your backyard garden. Picture fairies sitting softly on a branch of blossoms. Then imagine twirling yourself small and hopping up to join them, as all of you sway in the breeze and inhale the delightful scent of flowers. Fairies have names and personalities, just like you do. Let me tell you a bit about these two tiny, spritely creatures:

> Little TITTLES is the youngest,
> and she giggles as the blossoms tickle her feet.
> Sitting next to her is CHERRIE,
> a shy young fairy who picks bunches of flowers
> to crown her hair.

Be constantly inspired every day, even by the smallest things. The very fact of life itself is magical!

Lonely Dragon

Life can be sad, but don't despair.

You may feel forlorn and blue, abandoned by the very people you relied on. A great emptiness fills your soul, as you retreat within. But stop and reflect. Don't give up and retreat all by yourself to a gloomy castle high atop a cragged mountain!

These depressing times of life can serve as a valuable time of introspection. It will give you the opportunity to think about your goals and actions, and to plan what you will do in the future to make things better. Make this a rejuvenating experience, and you will surprise yourself by solving problems and planning a bright future ahead.

Mad Hatter's Tea Party

Celebrate life every day!

Be happy and enjoy the amazing variety and flavors of life. Be whimsical and see the humor and fantasy of existence. Make every day an "un-birthday party" (except on *your* birthday, of course!) You're never too old to play "games of imagining." So let's go!

Close your eyes and envision the delight of actually being at a tea party with some of your favorite fairy-tale characters, such as Alice, the Mad Hatter, and the March Hare. Then try this again and again with more of your cherished childhood storybook friends. Join in with their fun-filled Adventure, courtesy of your colorful imagination. Your personality will sparkle again. Being "childlike" can keep you forever young.

Magical Lands

Visit enchantment.

Change your perspective on life, and experience new adventures. Even though it might not be possible for you to actually travel to foreign lands and see amazing sights, you can do it through your fertile imagination.

Stories depicting fantastic places can "fly you away" to realms beyond your everyday life. If you immerse yourself into these new and exciting worlds, it will give you a sparkling view of life that will put a gleam in your eye and a bounce in your step. Feel the excitement!

Merlin and Young Arthur

Listen to your inspirational spiritual teachers.

It's always good to try your hand at being self-taught. But the gift of being inspired by great teachers of the past and present is an additional wonderful way to develop your talents to the fullest.

The amazing magician Merlin taught young Arthur the wizardly arts, and knowledge of all nature. Then Arthur became a great king. He had innate knowledge, which his teacher helped him develop to the utmost. You too have been born with wonderful abilities. Seek out teacher guides, even if they lived in the past. Study their works, in the forest of enchantment. They will take your hand and open up the world of miracles to you. Believe in yourself!

Moon Fairy Goddess

You too are lovely and kind.

When you create a "Mind Painting" of your ideal self, picture yourself as a great beauty. Aspire to become lovely in mind, body, and soul to the best of your abilities. You will thoroughly enjoy the new "you," and so will others. Here is a description of how you can picture and feel yourself transforming:

> Sit gracefully upon the crescent moon,
> Glowing and glistening in the evening sky.
> Be attended by fluttering butterflies and sparkling stars.
> You will then appear as the moon fairy goddess,
> Who is the guardian of magical wishes and secret dreams.

Make your secret dreams and wishes become reality!

Morning Glory Fairy

Discover the innocence and beauty of flowers.

Flowers teach us many things, such as the love of beauty. If you look closely enough among the blossoms, you may find some tiny, delicate fairies. They seem to be shy at first, but if you talk softly to them, they will become your friends and teach you secrets of their magical world. Here are some of the adorable qualities of the loving little morning glory fairy that may be helpful to you:

> First to wake at dawn of day is this perky,
> sweet-faced little fae.
>
> Then when her flowers start to stir,
> she lovingly hugs them close to her.
>
> And now this morning glory miss,
> upon each blossom plants a kiss.

Mounting Pegasus

Ascend to great heights.

Experiencing loss is a tragic thing. Shedding tears is very necessary to release sorrow and express your feelings. When you have felt the pain of despair deeply, you can now ride on the back of your trusty friend who guards your soul. He is Pegasus, the exuberant and beautiful creature who will fly you through the sky and beyond the moon!

Here you will visit sparkling stars, which give you reason and meaning to continue on with your wondrous life. When you return to Earth once again, you will have renewed purpose to live life to the fullest and continue on with many more exciting adventures to come.

Oberon and Titania

There is discord—even in Fairyland.

You can mend any argument and disagreement you have with those you care about. Try talking together to iron out the problems between you. Life is too short not to be friends.

Even the king and queen of Fairyland have their little tiffs. But they eventually reconcile their differences. There are always happy endings in the kingdom of the fae. Sometimes we have to work hard to create happy endings in our land of the mortals.

Pan and Unicorn

Magical beings surround us.

Be honest and true to yourself and others throughout life, and you will be happy. No matter where you go or what you do, you will know that you have followed both your heart and your high ideals. And because of this, you will be rewarded by realizing your dreams. They are symbolized by the beautiful white unicorn. Call your companion to you with melodious pipes, and he will come, in the twilight forest of reveries.

They say that celestial beings such as these are extinct. But they still do exist, in a higher dimension, where our hopes and aspirations dwell. The world is an amazing place. Get out of your feelings of the mundane and humdrum. You can create your own world of fantasy in your fertile imagination. Open up your eyes and you will discover an amazing reality, beyond anything you have ever experienced. You just have to know where to look.

Paradise of Children

Imagine your dreamworld.

In the Greek myth of Pandora, before she opened the fateful box and let the evil troubles out, the world was a peaceful and tranquil place. It was a paradise of children, where no one grew old, and everyone lived in harmony with each other and all of nature. You too can create your own perfect world within your mind. Sit quietly with your eyes closed, and picture a land where all is perfection. Create a beautiful, fantastic place where life is full of adventure, fun, and beauty, just the way you would like it to be.

So whenever you wish to escape the everyday world, you can just visit your special imaginary paradise. Then try to make your everyday world into a paradise too.

Peaceful Garden

Send healing thoughts.

You may feel overcome by sadness when you hear news of environmental disasters, war, and sickness. World events can be very depressing indeed. But keep hope alive in your heart and send out loving vibrations throughout the universe. Try visualizing the image described here, and then be creative to imagine your own tender visions:

> In a quiet moonlit garden,
> Send out two doves of peace
> To fly throughout the world,
> Spreading heartfelt love and kindness to all.
> Then meditate on the healing waters in your fountain of life,
> So that it can nourish and regenerate the Earth
> to become pure again.

Penguin Riding By

Laughter lets the sunshine in.

Don't forget the great healing power of humor. When you smile and give a chuckle, it creates a wonderful mood deep inside, which permeates throughout your entire mind and body. So try to experience the joy in life. It will make you feel wonderful, youthful, and give you a positive attitude.

Be imaginative and creative by thinking of funny people and incongruous situations, such as a "horseback-riding penguin all dressed up as a princess!" And I'm sure you can even do better than that one! Enjoy a big laugh! Watch a comedy. Giggle at little puppies playing tag. Have fun!

Puck's Magic Flower of Sleep

Understand the messages given you in dreams.

Dreams have symbolic messages, which can be fascinating clues to your mind, if you can just find the key to unlock the answers. Often you can't remember your dreams when you wake in the morning. If not, try to relax and remember any feelings and sensations about them if you can.

When you are able, recall some details of a dream; write down anything that may come to mind about what the symbols mean to you. You know your own mind better than anyone. And so you will be able to decipher personal messages your Guardian Spirits may have given you in your intricate and sometimes complicated night visions.

Share Some Joy

Give a bouquet of cheer.

Give a bouquet of cheer, a warm smile, and some kind and caring words. Exchange your hopes and dreams. Lend a sympathetic ear. You will receive warm feelings in return—of friendship and happiness—that will make your life full of joy.

The most important thing is not to give monetary wealth. It's the riches in your loving heart that will be the most appreciated by everyone who receives your kindness. And they will thank you by sharing their kindness with you.

Sleeping Beauty

Awaken to the love of life.

Long have you slumbered, covered over by brambles and vines, unaware of your great potential and beauty. But soon you will awaken by the loving kiss of life, which will rejuvenate you from the lingering sleep of winter.

Then rise and shine and wipe away the cobwebs! Blossom into glorious springtime and become the beautiful being that has lain dormant deep inside your soul!

Teddy Bear Picnic

Enjoy a delicious garden party with friends.

On a warm spring day, join your friends in the fresh air for a delightful tea party picnic. Food always tastes scrumptious outdoors, on a sunny day among the flowers.

When you eat, be sure to relish and enjoy every bite, chewing it slowly to digest it well. Eat food that is as healthy, organic, and unprocessed as possible, with no harmful additives or preservatives. Cut down on sugary sweets, and drink fruit juice, good water, and herbal teas. Green tea with honey is wonderful, as is eating lots of fresh fruits and vegetables. Improving your eating habits might help heal other health problems you may have as well. A positive mental attitude also contributes to well-being. Be happy!

The Lovers

Make your happy endings.

You will always be a romantic. Your soulmate is with you always. If you haven't found one yet, never give up your search. Some day soon you will find your dream.

Life does not have to be mournful and sad if you keep a positive attitude and hope of finding true love.

The Magic Flute

Listen to the lilting music of Pan.

Music can transport you to other worlds. The entire realm of art plays an important part in everyone's life, so that we may feel uplifted and inspired to higher realms. Let go of your preconceived notions that fantasy is just for the young. We will all remain "young at heart" if we believe in the magical power of art to unleash our imaginations and make us more fulfilled as human beings.

So listen to the soothing and uplifting strains of music as much as you can. Let it surround you and transport you to celestial realms:

> Off in the distance is a castle of clouds,
> Made from dreams of all who listen to the music of Pan.

The Road to Oz

Stay on your path.

You are well on the road to achieving your lofty goals. Stay the course. Believe in yourself. You might meet good and evil along the way, and your path may have stumbling blocks. But that's a part of life. Various aspects of yourself will be your faithful companions along the way: your mind, heart, and courage of spirit.

The Yellow Brick Road of life is a great adventure into unknown realms. But remember, if you click the heels of your ruby slippers three times, you can always return home. And you will be the richer for having had your amazing exploits.

Touch of Angels

Celestial healing powers are within you.

Sublime Angelic Beings have spiritual ways to restore our mind, body, and spirit. You have a natural potential for transcendental restoration within you, if you will just believe in your abilities. The soothing touch of your warm, vibrant hands, and your ability to send healing thoughts and vibrations throughout the world, may be yet untapped. You can develop these talents and other similar gifts if you study this realm. It is very satisfying to be able to help speed the healing process of yourself and others. There are several exciting fields to investigate along these lines, such as meditation, therapeutic touch, massage, etc. Many of these methods are based on ancient practices that have been handed down from civilizations long ago.

You can also work along with a good healer to get personalized guidance. These spiritual healing methods can of course be used in conjunction with excellent MDs and DOs who treat illnesses and provide preventive care. Visualize your Guardian Angels and ask them for guidance as to what path to take.

Tulip Fairy

Play games of wonder with the fairies.

You may feel sad and lonely now, because things aren't working out well for you. Why not ask help from little elves and fairies? You might be surprised to learn that they know a lot about being happy and making life full of sparkles! Hop into your garden of imagination, where you can confide in these whimsical sprites. They most certainly will give you some delightful suggestions, since they love to help humans. Here is what the tiny Fairy of the Tulips does to have fun: She dresses up in pretty colors, which puts a bloom on her cheeks and a smile on her lips. Then she flits and flies about visiting her little flower fairy friends, happily playing hide-and-seek among the brightly colored blossoms.

If you open your heart to the Wee Folk, they will pop ideas into your head to cheer you. Fly out of the darkness and into the light, and feel the sunshine!

Welcome to Make-Believe

Step into your dreams.

Remember your youth, and what made you happy. This joy can be rekindled in your mind, since these feelings are still within you. They may just have been covered over in your process of growing up. Imagine yourself innocent as a child again, and enter into the world of storybook dreams, by playing an imaginary game such as this one:

Close your eyes, and step into a "dreamworld." Feel that your dream is very real—as real as you experience your everyday world to be. Breathe deeply to inhale the delightful scents of a magical garden of giant flowers. Then envision a fantastic world of make-believe, filled with as many amazing creatures as you can conjure up. Your vision will be unforgettable, with the possibility of many more exciting ones to come. See a glowing fairy touch your hand and welcome you to believe in make-believe.

Where Candy Trees Grow

*Lands of childhood live within us
always throughout life.*

Never give up these visions. Always reach for the sweetest sugarplums, high up in the candy trees of your imagination. Fairy tales and poems that we have read when we were young will always remain in our memories, even if we think we have forgotten them. Try to remember and bring them forth. By reading them again, a warm and happy feeling of delight and youth will well up inside you.

Never let go of your childhood dreams and fun. It will keep you always young in mind and heart.

Wizard of the Galaxy

Experience the magic of the universe!

You will never be bored if you strive to develop your innate powers of imagination. One way is to create mind-expanding experiences, which are extremely uplifting and inspiring. For instance, how would you like to witness the magical creation of a universe?

Sit in your secret quiet place, making the lights dim. Begin by breathing deeply and concentrating on your body, relaxing and letting go of all built-up tensions. Hold an object that you can meditate on, such as a glass ball, or just gaze at a blank wall. As you focus your attention, visualize the darkness of outer space, with glowing stars and planets. Imagine the flickering star lights glowing brighter and brighter. Then picture an imposing being appearing who creates a universe full of color and life! A galaxy is born!

*You can become your own magician
and continue to create and experience
many of your own original
Inspirational Visions.*